Covenant UNDER FIRE
WHAT THE ENEMY REALLY WANTS

by

CHRISTOPHER L. WALKER

Unless otherwise indicated, all Scripture quotations are taken from the Amplified Version of the bible.
Some quotations are taken from the New Living Translation, New King James, King James, Message, NIV, NASB, GW and Amplified Version of the bible.

1st Printing

Covenant Under Fire: What The Enemy Really Wants!
ISBN 978-0692803226

Copyright © 2016 by Christopher Walker International
P.O. Box 120337
Clermont, FL 34712 www.cathedralofpower.org

Published by
Innovative Creative Enterprise (ICE) Media Group
P.O. Box 120337
Clermont, FL 34712

Printed in the United States of America. All rights reserved under International Copyright Law. This book or parts thereof may not be reproduced in any form, stored in a retrieval system, or transmitted in any form by any means- electronic, mechanical, photocopy, recording, or otherwise- without prior written permission of the publisher, except as provided by United States of America copyright law.

Book Cover Design & Interior Layout amd design by:
Fellowship Media
fellowshipMedia.net | 407-434-9680

Editorial Services by: Bertha Coleman

CONTENTS

	Forward	1
	Endorsements	3

CHAPTERS

1	The Essence of Covenant	8
2	CHURCH: The Sleeping Giant	23
3	War on Christianity	35
4	Authority Under Fire	39
5	Morality in Decline	44
6	Family and Marriage Redefined	52
7	War on Wisdom	60
8	Renewing Our First Love	70

FORWARD

For decades now this nation has been teetering on the brink of moral and spiritual decadence. What was once a nation built on foundations that seemed steady and sure, has now become a nation standing in sinking sand. The Bible declares that if the foundations be destroyed, what can the righteous do? That seems to be the question. What can we do? Where do we go from here? How can we get it back? Is there still hope? The answer is yes! But we must arise and put on the whole armor of God and fight, for we are truly living in an age of Re-definition. Where there has been a systematic attempt by the adversary to destroy and remove from this nation and the church, the very absolutes and principles that we were built on.

If you are truly concerned about the direction of this world receive the Prophetic instructions in this Book. This book is directional; it is also a Kingdom Manuel and a refreshing word to the church. If my people, which are called by my name, shall humble themselves, and pray, and seek my face, and turn from their wicked ways; then will I hear from heaven, and will forgive their sin, and will heal their land 2 Chronicles Chapter 7 Verse 14. Yes, it will question your commitment to God, the world and your families. Will you be one of those that will rise and speak God's Word in a time of chaos?

In his book Covenant Under Fire Chris Walker boldly accepts the mantel and responsibility, to call this nation back to its original God intended purpose. With great accuracy he describes, identifies, and addresses the issues that are plaguing our nation and the church. And then with prophetic precision, he declares to us what the righteous must do to see the redemption of the land. This is truly a book and a man who has come to the kingdom for such a time as this!

Dr. Isaac Pitre, Founder Christ Nations Church Texarkana, Texas

ENDORSEMENTS

Pastor Chris Walker unapologetically speaks the veracity of the Word of God to legislative officials, community forums and ministries throughout America and abroad. Pastor Chris Walker's book, Covenant Under Fire boldly addresses hard-core issues regarding our faith and society. Covenant Under Fire exposes the systemic blueprint in our society to dismantle the core values of our faith. Pastor Chris Walker challenges every leader to uphold Romans 1:16 For I am not ashamed of the gospel of Christ: for it is the power of God unto salvation to everyone that believeth; to the Jew first, and also to the Greek. Covenant Under Fire, will motivate and inspire you to preserve your position of authority as a believer; and contend earnestly for the faith! - **Dr. Riva Tims Author "When It All Falls Apart" & "When It All Comes Together." Majestic Life Church - Orlando, FL**

"Covenant Under Fire is a must-read book for anyone concerned about the moral decline of our nation and how the Church can turn things around." - **Anthony Verdugo, Founder and Executive Director, Christian Family Coalition (CFC) Florida**

"Covenant Under Fire is a solid guide of truth that takes readers on a journey of God's covenant that affirms his love and promises to his people. I was moved and inspired as this book reinforces the uniqueness of our personal relationship with God; confirming who we are in him and who He is in us. The author reminds us of how essential it is to explore the word of God for ourselves, so we are not deceived nor blindsided by the lies and attacks of the enemy. Pastor Chris walker does an incredible job outlining our position and God's promise for such a time as now." - ***LaVeda M. Jones Author of Raising A Prince Without A King***

In every Generation before there is a major shift, in Government, Politics, Morally, Socially and Economically. God will prepare a vessel and release a Prophetic Voice to prepare, educate, sound an alarm and give direction to his people. God has truly answered so many prayers that many are secretly praying in their private chambers, concerning the question WHY. Why are we seeing our country, communities, families and even our churches in the chaos that we are seeing? God has answered that question and given Prophetic strategy to the church, government and the world through this book Covenant Under Fire. – ***Pastor Eryk E. Anglin, Author "I BELIEVE: Releasing the Supernatural" Ambassadors International Ministries***

Today's society is filled with ridiculing the church and the people of God. Many Christians have fallen away to the lust of the world and the sabotagement of their relationship with their savior. However, God has strategically ordained leaders to be on the frontline to boldly proclaim God's principles. With an unwavering voice, these people will not bow down to Baal or his doctrines. They are not afraid to stand up for the word of God. Though ostracized and attacked for their beliefs, they have adamantly adhered to the truth. They are the modern day watchmen and prophets who speak as a sound of a trumpet preparing the people of God. They are the Pastor Chris Walkers of the world whom God has anointed to lead the people back to their first love thus restoring their relationship with God. Yes the covenant is under fire with God and his people. However, this book will show you how to protect your bond with God in a world that has lost its zeal for God's love. - ***Apostle Veryl Howard Matthew 6:33 Global Min. Faith Management & Talent Casting***

Covenant Under Fire is a must read book. It is what God is saying to the Church and season we live in. This book is explosive, candid, and an eye-opener. It allows the reader to feel the heart- beat of God. **- Dr. Ephantus Steve Ngigi – Kenya Africa**

As life values and lifestyle norms are being eradicated and erased from the map of society it is crucial that we as God's covenant people take these words to heart. Covenant Under Fire is an important and essential read for this season. **– Pastor Christian Hedegaard, Powerhouse Church Orlando, Florida**

This is very well stated and I think the book is a timely message... Great work Pastor Chris **– Pastor Jerone Davis – Retired NFL**

Ezekiel 22:30 says "God is looking for someone who will build the wall and stand in the gap." There is definitely a cloud of deception sweeping the church concerning righteousness and it is affecting the state of our nation. Thank you Chris for your courage to be someone who will "build a wall and stand in the gap **- Dr. Faith Fredrick; President Faith Christian University Orlando, FL**

'In an hour where it is exceedingly unpopular to stand upon traditional Judaeo Christian values and principles, Pastor Chris Walker dares to tread against mainstream philosophy and challenge modern America, the Church and western culture at large to undergo a critical reexamination of its developmental path. In 'Covenant Under Fire', Walker calls for America and the Church to inspect its biblical foundation. **- Ambassador Devon Rolle Founder, Sr. Pastor Kingdom Discipleship Center Nassau, Bahamas**

"THEN GOD SAID, "I AM GIVING YOU A SIGN OF MY COVENANT WITH YOU AND WITH ALL LIVING CREATURES, FOR ALL GENERATIONS TO COME. I HAVE PLACED MY RAINBOW IN THE CLOUDS. IT IS THE SIGN OF MY COVENANT WITH YOU AND WITHALL THE EARTH."

Genesis 9:11-13 NLT

CHAPTER 1
The Essence of Covenant

A Covenant is a promise, pledge, or treaty. It's a sacred covenant agreement between God and a person or group of people. God sets specific conditions, and He promises to bless us as we obey those conditions. When we choose not to keep covenants, we cannot receive the blessings, and in some instances we suffer a penalty as a consequence of our disobedience.

Covenants mark the path back to God. It is similar in meaning to the idea of "contract", although the two words are not perfectly synonymous, and the differences between them are significant.

In the ancient Middle East where the Bible was written), a covenant was a formal agreement that caused (or implied) several things:

First, a covenant defined (or sometimes created) a relationship. This relationship might be between a king and his vassal states, between a deity and his nation, or between two humans, etc.

Second, some covenants are conditional (if one party does "A", then the other party will do "B"), just as with a present-day contract. But generally, ancient covenants are unconditional (each party commits to a certain action, regardless of whether the other party keeps the covenant).

Third, covenants often included the slaughter of animals as a symbol of their significance.

Forth, unlike present-day contracts, covenants often carried no expiration date. Thus the parties were understood to be bound by the covenant until death (or forever, in the case of covenants with God).

Fifth, a contract is enforced by the civil government; a covenant is regulated by God.

Six, a contract involves the exchange of property or actions; a covenant binds two parties together personally.

The Nature of the Covenant

There is much ignorance and confusion among professed Christians concerning the covenant. Even though I do not intend to contest all kinds of inaccurate teachings about the covenant, I warn that there are serious errors on the doctrine of the covenant, not only in the evangelical churches, but also in most churches. It has become plain that these errors concerning the covenant fatally compromise the gospel of salvation by the grace of God in Jesus Christ alone. Particularly, the fundamental doctrine of justification by faith alone is corrupted and denied.

The covenant of God with His people is a unique relationship of intimate fellowship in mutual love. That was the covenant announced to Adam and Eve in the garden immediately after the fall. That was the covenant established with Abraham. That was the covenant as administered to Israel, even though the covenant with Israel was burdened with the law. This is the nature of the perfect form of the covenant with believers and our children in the present, gospel age.

We must not think of the covenant as comparable to a bargain struck by two businessmen, dependent upon stipulated conditions, for the purpose of the advantage of them both. But we must think of the covenant of God with men and women as a delightful marriage, or as a warm friendship. It should be evident at once that keeping the covenant makes a world of difference, whether we think of the covenant between God and us as a cold, business-like, conditional bargain, or as comparable to a marriage or friendship. A spouse and a friend behave differently than a businessman, especially with regard to the motives of the heart.

There is a loss of covenant consciousness among Christians. Covenant Conscience is a term that describes an aspect of a human being's self-awareness. It is part of a person's internal rational capacity and is not, as popular lore sometimes suggests, an audience room for the voice of God or of the devil. Conscience is a critical inner awareness that bears witness to the norms and values we recognize and apply. The complex of values with which conscience deals, includes not only those we own, but the entire range of values to which we are exposed during life's journey. Consequently, there is always a sense of struggle in our reflective process. The witness of conscience makes its presence known by inducing mental anguish and feelings of guilt when we violate the values we recognize and apply. Conscience also provides a sense of pleasure when we reflect on conformity to our value system.

The covenant is of the greatest importance according to Scripture. When God began to work out the salvation of His people in the nation of Israel in the Old Testament—a work that would culminate in the coming of Jesus the Messiah and His redemption of God's people His covenant with Abraham and his seed (Genesis 12). It is necessary that we know that all the blessings we have from God are covenant blessings. What husband would be pleased that his wife received all his love, care, and gifts while remaining oblivious to the marriage in which he lavished his love upon her? God's love, salvation, and care come to His people in and on behalf of the covenant, which is the real marriage.

As will become plain when we see what the covenant is, God already revealed the covenant in the very first promise of the Gospel, in Genesis 3:15: "And I will put enmity between thee and the woman, and between thy seed and her seed; it shall bruise thy head, and thou shalt bruise his heel." This importance of the covenant lends urgency to our calling to keep the covenant.

Today there are a lot of leaders and Christians in the news because of scandal, deception, divorce, babies out of wedlock, and extra-marital affairs, but yet they are still in ministry, and they look like they are doing well. And we are being tricked into thinking that it is okay with God because no one has held them accountable. Sexual perversion is at an all-time high. Divorce among Christians is at a high. Hollywood is telling us that marriage is a thing of the past, and it has become socially acceptable for a man and a woman to live together without being married. It is said that they are trying to get to know one another and to see if they are sexually compatible.

Mothers are abandoning their children and new born babies at record numbers. Husbands are abusing and killing their wives in order to be with someone else. Politicians are being exposed on corruption and moral failure almost monthly. School teachers are molesting our children and even women are having babies by their students. The murder rate is up in various cities around the nation, and everyone is asking what is going on.

The answer to the question of what is going on is this: OUR COVENANT WITH GOD IS UNDER FIRE!

1 Chronicles 16:15 (NLT) says *"Remember his covenant forever— the commitment he made to a thousand generations"*. God doesn't want us to forget the covenants that He has made to His children. The covenant refers to the Word that God spoke. This is why we refer to the Bible as a testament or covenant. And the words which He spoke are the scriptures upon which we base our relationship with our Heavenly Father. In Romans 1:25-27 (NASB) Paul lists the many aspects of a sinful character and a sinful society that has broken its covenant with God. He says, "For they exchanged the truth of God for a lie, and worshiped and served the creature rather than the Creator, who is blessed forever. Amen.

For this reason God gave them over to degrading passions; for their women exchanged the natural function for that which is unnatural, and in the same way also the men abandoned the natural function of the woman and burned in their desire toward one another, men with men committing indecent acts and receiving in their own persons the due penalty of their error."

Paul mentions the sins of breaking the covenant. In a sense, covenant breaking is the foundation for all sin. The greatest sin that Paul mentions is that they have exchanged the truth about God for a lie and worshipped idols created by man. We live in a time where people don't want the truth, and choose to create their own truth. Keeping commitment is no longer a priority. A man who fathers children, and then leaves the family is a renegade father. He has broken the trust of his wife and children; he has turned away from his covenant responsibility.

God always keeps His covenant with and we have to learn how to keep our covenant with Him because He wants nothing but life and favor for His children. Proverbs 8:35 says, "For he who finds me finds life and obtains favor from the Lord." So the issue remains: Why is the devil after our covenant?

To answer that question we must first understand the root of Satan's problem which is found in the book of Ezekiel 28:11-18 (GW). He said, "Son of man, sing a funeral song for the ruler of Tyre. Tell him, 'This is what the Almighty Lord says: You were the perfect example, full of wisdom and perfect in beauty. You were in Eden, God's garden. You were covered with every kind of precious stone: red quartz, topaz, crystal, beryl, onyx, gray quartz, sapphire, turquoise, and emerald. Your settings and your sockets were made of gold when you were created. I appointed an angel[a] to guard you. You were on God's holy mountain. You walked among fiery stones.

Your behavior was perfect from the time you were created, until evil was found in you. You traded far and wide. You learned to be violent, and you sinned. So I threw you down from God's mountain in disgrace. The guardian angel forced you out from the fiery stones. You became too proud because of your beauty. You wasted your wisdom because of your greatness. So I threw you to the ground and left you in front of the kings so that they could see you. You dishonored your own holy places because of your many sins and dishonest trade. So I set fire to you to burn you up. I turned you into ashes on the ground in the presence of all who saw you."

Everywhere Lucifer walked praises were given to God and glory was created. Lucifer controlled the glory. He was the one who led and created an atmosphere for God's presence. He had full access to all levels in heaven. He was allowed to the holy mountain where God resided. What would have consumed most angels, God allowed him to be able to withstand. He defiled his covenant relationship because he thought he was better than God and deceived a third of the angels to follow him. The text says that Lucifer was in the Garden of Eden first before man was created. God created Adam because he was void of any covenant relationship. He did with man what he never did with Lucifer and any other angel. He made us in his image to be just like him.

So understand this: Satan hates us because every time we praise God we remind him of his old job and covenant that he lost. Every time he sees us he sees the image of the God he broke covenant with. So when Adam came along in the Garden of Eden he wanted man to lose his covenant! Know that the enemy is upset with you and me because we became his replacements under a better covenant. So he *is* after your promise and your purpose .When I looked up the word *covenant* it said *"promise"* and when I looked up the word *promise* it said *"potential, possibilities"*. So in essence Satan is still mad at losing the purpose and potential of his former promise.

In the Book of Job we see Satan going to and fro until he is asked by God if he had considered Job. At first Satan doesn't want the challenge as he is aware of the covenantal protection that Job is under. So he challenges God to lift the protection, but God only gives him partial access to test Job. Satan really didn't care about Job's kids, his wife, his wealth or his friends—Satan wanted Job's covenant protection with God.

Hebrews 8:10-12 (NLT) says, "But this is the new covenant I will make with the people of Israel on that day, says the Lord: I will put my laws in their minds, and I will write them on their hearts. I will be their God, and they will be my people. And they will not need to teach their neighbors, nor will they need to teach their relatives, saying, 'You should know the Lord. For everyone, from the least to the greatest, will know me already. And I will forgive their wickedness, and I will never again remember their sins."

God wants and desires more of a relationship with His people. He wants to commune with us daily, not just when we need something. The enemy is upset because he lost. God looked at Lucifer after he fell and said, *"I am going to do something that I have never done before and won't do again, I am going to make man in my image and deposit a part of me inside of him. I am going to breathe my DNA into him."* The spirit of God dwells on the inside of us. That is why you and I are in a spiritual war! You remind the devil of his daddy!

When asked if people believe in the devil, some people believe there is an evil force, but do not have a clue where it comes from. Others believe there is a devil, but they do not fully understand his powers or abilities. John 10:10 exposes the devil's intent for us. *"The thief's purpose is to steal and kill and destroy. My purpose is to give them a rich and satisfying life."*

His plan for you is total destruction. The enemy has caused great men and women throughout history to fall and fail. Even Adam and Eve, two people who had an ongoing covenant relationship with God every day, allowed a reject from heaven, to denounce the word of God and question what God had declared. Don't allow the devil or sin to steal what God has given you. Don't let him steal your covenant!

Someone once said, "Sin will take you places you don't want to go, sin will keep you longer than you wanted to stay, and it will make you pay a price you thought you could not afford or were willing to pay." "Jesus said that He came that you might have LIFE and have it more abundantly."

JESUS CAME TO RESTORE THE COVENANT.

In Matthew Chapter 4 Jesus was led to pray (this is why the devil tried to tempt him after he had fasted for 40 days in the wilderness and offer him dominion that He already had!) Man shall not live on materialism or desires alone but by the covenant that proceeds out of the mouth of God.

Colossians 3 says, "Set your affections on things above." The reason I don't go to the club any more drink no more, walk in greed or envy is because I have set my affections on things above that are found in my new covenant.

But covenant unlike most contracts, goes on from one generation to the next. God desires for His promises to extend from your children to your grandchildren and to every generation succeeding forever after. There are many covenants that God has with us and for us. I can't list all of them as this book would be too long to read but here are a few.

A Grace Covenant

Established in Christ, the covenant is gracious. It is truly the "covenant of grace," as Scripture names it. It is not a covenant of human works, of human will, or of human worth.

God decreed the covenant in His eternal counsel, out of

grace alone. God confirmed the covenant in the cross of Christ, out of grace alone. God establishes the covenant in the hearts of elect believers and the genuine children of believers—the "children of the promise" (Rom. 9:8) —by the regenerating Spirit, out of grace alone. God maintains the covenant and perfects it with all those who are Christ's, preserving His covenant friends, out of grace alone.

The covenant is unconditional: it does not depend upon the sinner. The teaching that the covenant is conditional is a form of the denial of salvation by grace alone. This doctrine makes salvation in the covenant a matter of man's willing and running, which Romans 9:16 rejects: *"it is not of him that willeth, nor of him that runneth."* In light of what the covenant is, namely, fellowship between God and His people, fellowship established in Christ, and fellowship that is gracious, we can understand rightly what Scripture means when it admonishes us to keep the covenant.

Evangelism as a Covenant

Evangelism is the act of love in the sense that it seeks to restore a relationship that is broken. An unsaved person is alienated from his relationship with God. Evangelism confronts a person with the blood covenant offered by Jesus. The sinner in return is invited by this loving confrontation to reenter a relationship with God and other believers in the world.

Deuteronomy 7:9 says, *"GOD IS FAITHFUL TO KEEP COVENANT WITH THOSE WHO ARE FAITHFUL TO KEEP COVENANT WITH HIM."*

We must understand that there is no reason for God to perform any action for us outside of covenant. Not only does God refuse to act outside of covenant, but He is legally not allowed to. Covenant bears with it a restriction on outside activity. Ez 20:37 states that God's desire toward Israel was to: "make you pass under the rod and bring you into the bond of the covenant."

In a covenant one commits themselves not to act outside of the boundaries of that relationship. In a marriage, the man and woman commits themselves not to have relations with others. (forsaking all others!)

Prophecy as a Covenant

Amos 3:3 the question is asked, *"Can two walk together unless they are agreed?"* The answer is "NO". God cannot walk on this earth unless He does so in cooperation with an earth citizen. To walk together they must come into covenant agreement. God will not act outside His covenant with a human being. *"Surely the Lord God does nothing, unless He reveals His secret to His servants the prophets,"* (Amos 3:7). The prophets in this passage are representative partners of God's covenant. God will not act unless He comes into agreement with his partners on the earth. David states in Psalm 25:14 (NLT), "The Lord is a friend to those who fear him."

God extends revelation to a group of human beings in response to and in agreement of a covenant with them. Everything that GOD does is wrapped up in covenant keeping. We are ambassadors from God. We are brokers of the new covenant. We are legal witnesses in evangelism, bringing an official testimony to the other person. God's way of salvation through Jesus may be seen as an act of covenant. Evangelism is a call for covenantal reconciliation to our God. - 2 Cor 5:18

Prayer as a Covenant

The purpose of prayer is to establish an action in the earth based upon a covenant agreement between God and His human partner. Prayer itself is an act of exercising covenant. Matthew 18:19 (NLT) indicates that prayers to God in faith are done on the basis of covenantal agreement. *"I also tell you this: If two of you agree here on earth concerning anything you ask, my Father in heaven will do it for you."* Prayer is an agreement with a partner on earth with his partner in heaven. When the corporate church body or a family comes together on the same page, agreeing for the power of God to move in their lives, the unexplainable takes place because of covenant.

Prosperity as a Covenant

Deuteronomy 8:18 (ESV) "You shall remember the Lord your God, for it is he who gives you power to get wealth, that he may confirm his covenant that he swore to your fathers, as it is this day." All wealth originally comes from God, and only those who are in covenant with Him have a right to have it. God said to Abraham, "I am blessing you to be a blessing!"

Please know that God's greatest desire is that our spiritual soul prospers first. "3 John 1:2 (King James Version) Beloved, I wish above all things that thou mayest prosper and be in health, even as thy soul prospereth.

The Necessity of Keeping the Covenant

Although not a work of man upon which the covenant depends, keeping the covenant is important, indeed, necessary. It is necessary, because God demands it, because it is the way in which we are saved, and know we are saved, and because it glorifies God, which is the chief end of the covenant.

But covenant keeping is necessary also in view of the fact that the covenant is a relationship of fellowship between God and us. We have a part in the covenant, just as God also has a part. In an earthly relationship, both of those who are related to each other must do their duty. The husband loves his wife and cares for her, and the wife submits to her husband and helps him. Parents rear their children in love, and the children honor their father and mother. So in the spiritual relationship of the covenant, God in Christ loves and saves His friends and children, according to His own free promise. His people love, reverence, serve, and obey Him, which is His demand of us and our calling.

Even though God works in us to do our part in the covenant, He works in such a way that we keep the covenant freely, willingly, cheerfully, and carefully. And this pleases God immensely, just as it pleases a husband that his wife loves him and is willingly helpful. It displeases God greatly, that we fail to keep the covenant. Therefore, He chastens His children for disobedience, sometimes severely.

In addition, it's so important to God for us to keep our covenant responsibilities that He tries, or tests, our commitment to Him. Such was the trial (not "temptation," in Genesis 22:1) of Abraham in the matter of offering Isaac to God as a sacrifice. When we pass the test, as Abraham did, God is pleased with us, as He was with Abraham: "for now I know that you truly fear God. You have not withheld from me even your son, your only son." (Gen. 22:12) NLT.

Many married couples after 20, 30, or 50 years of marriage have vow renewal ceremonies. This is a time to renew the vows that they made when they first got married. The couple reflects on all they have come to know and appreciate about each other. They remember the high and low seasons of their relationship and the trying times that they once faced. It's a time to rekindle their love for one another with new commitments.

As believers that experience ups and downs, highs and low seasons of faith, we need to come to the realization that our relationship with God needs a renewal, a recommitment to the covenant we first made. Much like people who have been married for 20 years and they do a vowel renewal ceremony. This is to re-state their commitment to each other. We can't allow the enemy to steal the promise that God has made to us. We can't afford for the enemy to move us from our ordained purpose much like he did with Adam in Eve in the Garden. Thank God for loving us so much that He sent His son Jesus to give us a new and better covenant.

"I LOOKED FOR SOMEONE WHO MIGHT REBUILD THE WALL OF RIGHTEOUSNESS THAT GUARDS THE LAND. I SEARCHED FOR SOMEONE TO STAND IN THE GAP IN THE WALL SO I WOULDN'T HAVE TO DESTROY THE LAND, BUT I FOUND NO ONE."

Ezekiel 22:30 NLT

CHAPTER 2
Church: The Sleeping Giant

In the book of Jonah Chapter One we learn about a prophet who God had called to speak and warn the people about how wicked they were living their lives. The City of Ninevah was a superpower of its day but they had become consumed with their own lusts and had turned away from living for God. Jonah was given an instruction by God to warn the people or they would incur judgment. But the prophet who knew God's voice, who knew God's will did not want to speak to the people and decided to run from his assignment.

He went to the City of Joppa and purchased a ticket on a cruise ship that was headed to Tarshish. Not long after the ship took off God sent a great wind on the sea, so they entered into a great storm and began to experience some major issues. The sailors on the ship were terrified and tried everything they could to keep the ship from breaking apart and sinking. But while all of this was going on Jonah had gone below deck, where he laid down and fell into a deep sleep.

The captain of the ship later went down and woke him up and asked the sleepy prophet, "How can you sleep at a time like this? Get up and call on your God so we don't perish!" I believe the world is saying the same thing to the Church today, *"How can you sleep at a time like this?"* The world is looking at a slumbering, divided church saying, "where are the true prophets of God, the ones that gave them truth that they could navigate by, and make it through the storms of life?" Where are the prophets who are more concerned about doing God's will then making money?

Where are the prophets who are more concerned about God's reputation than their celebrity status? Where are the true prophets of God that preach righteousness, holiness, separation from sin, sanctification and consecration? The storm is raging, the ship is going down, the ship is being destroyed, lives are being destroyed, our society is being destroyed. America is in an economic storm, society is in a moral storm and the church is in a spiritual storm.

We the Church are living in dangerous times. Today the righteous are deemed religious and the religious are called righteous. We no longer have the discernment in the Kingdom for deception. We celebrate anybody that claims they are Christian without clearly looking at their lifestyle. The Church is attacked for its stance on holiness and the world is praised for its ability to deceive the very elect. The church is divided because we chose to argue the scripture and not recognize who God really is. Hyper-Grace has destroyed the purity of the Church and made it an entertainment center and a place for small social groups.

Hyper Grace or False Grace gospel is a new wave teaching that distorts the Biblical teaching of Grace and presents only bits and pieces of scripture laying emphasis on one sided view of grace. Hyper Grace Teachers teach that the past, present and future sins of a person are already forgiven on the cross and there is no need to neither repent of our sins nor confess our sins. Instead they teach that phrase "Just Believe and be saved". They pick all their doctrines from the Bible, but the sad thing is they pick it totally out of context and put them all together and make a concocted doctrine. Anyone who disagrees with them is often labeled as a Legalist, Pharisee or as a man bound by religion.

The sad thing is the hyper grace teachers have formed a religion of their own and they are more careful to use their arguments in a religious manner. Hyper grace teachers often mock the evangelicals as "Hell fire preachers" and warn their followers not to be sin conscious. They stress on "Jesus Conscious" and the problem of sin is never addressed in their gospel. Whenever the hyper grace teachers come across a verse in the Bible that talk about repenting from sins, they would immediately say that particular verse was not written for believers. The Bible clearly talks about repenting from sin.

If we don't get back to basics *the Church* will be the reason why God judges this nation and *the Church*. The prophet Isaiah sounded out a warning to a generation like ours. In Isaiah 5:20, *"Woe unto them that call evil good, and good evil; that put darkness for light, and light for darkness; that put bitter for sweet, and sweet for bitter."*

- What was once called sin and an abomination unto God (homosexuality and lesbianism) is now simply called an alternative lifestyle.
- Murder of babies in the mother's womb is now called pro-choice.
- Alcoholism is not recognized as bondage or an addiction anymore; it's just called a disease.
- Fornication and adultery are not called sin anymore; they're just called indiscretions.
- Stealing is not called sin; it's now called "habit of environment" or excessive borrowing.

It is not a time to be spiritually asleep; it's time to be awake

and spiritually alert, so that we can aggressively and boldly confront the powers of darkness. Rom 13:11 *And that knowing the time it is high time to awake out of sleep for now is our salvation nearer than when we believed.*
How can we be asleep when the Word of God is being watered down, softened, and stripped of its power—when it's simply a feel good message to the ears.

I believe today just as the shipmaster came to wake up the sleeping prophet Jonah, the Holy Spirit, who is the ship master of the church, is sending a wakeup call today. Many big-named preachers are silent in their stances for righteousness. They have forgotten that God gave them a mega- platform not for their own popularity, but to declare the Gospel to those that don't know Him. Some, when given the opportunity, to declare what God's word says on national news media, cave-into the same way of thinking of the humanistic culture that we live in.

God's people and lost souls are our business!

Finally the prophet Jonah realized that he, not the world, was the problem concerning why things had gotten so bad. The Church must take responsibility for some of this turmoil that our nation is in. When Jonah woke out of his sleep souls were saved because a slumbering prophet decided to wake up. Jonah woke up to his calling and he woke up to responsibility. It's time for the Church to wake up; we can longer have a Kermit the Frog mentality and say, "It's none of my Business; God's people and lost souls are our business!

The evidence is weighty and undeniable—Western Christian religion is crumbling, its authority and influence is fading, its adherents are disengaging. The erosion started slowly, but has picked up steam. Christianity as we know it is becoming irrelevant. Jesus commanded us to reach out into the sinful world and share the good news of the gospel of salvation. But He also warned us to not conform to the deception and lies of the world. Some believe the "identity crisis" within many professing Christians is a good thing– that it is causing the church to "re-think" its mission and purpose.

Others view this confusion as a license to "secularize" the church and marginalize the eternal truth of God and His Word. During the last 30 years our American culture has moved far away from its fundamental biblical values and principles. Secularism is simply leaving God out and most Americans today are secularists. The idea of a sovereign, holy, personal God is no longer a foundational mindset for most Americans. They have no fear of God. Even if He exists they do not believe He engages man in time and history. Eighty five percent of our children attend public, government run schools, which for the last three generations have gradually silenced a biblical worldview and presented life without God.

Something had to take God's place as the purpose and reason for living and it has become man himself. Humanism is putting man at the center of life rather than God. While the Bible teaches us to love God even to the contempt of self, humanism teaches us to love self even to the contempt of God. America has steadily moved toward a humanistic way of life.

The final characteristic of modern American thought and behavior concerns our morality and decision making. The decision-making of our culture is not generally based on unchanging biblical principles but on personal circumstances. The idea of absolute truth coming from a holy God has become absurd to most Americans. The idea that there are absolute standards of moral conduct is not part of their mindset. They innately believe that circumstances and personal desires are the only factors in making life's choices. This is called relativism.

There are not absolute standards for relativists. Truth and moral conduct is relative – it depends on the situation. For example, abortion, deviant sexual orientation, and abandoning marital commitments, are not wrong since there is no ultimate right and wrong in their worldview.
This secular, humanistic, and relativistic way of life is the very opposite of a biblical approach. Christians are taught to put Christ in, put Him at the center, and make His truth absolute—not put Him out, put a man at the center, and make truth relative.

Thirty years ago much of the secular part of our culture still thought and behaved in ways consistent with a biblical world view. This is no longer true. The divide has become so great that it has forced believers to make difficult choices in nearly every area and relationship.

The creation of the mixed Church to bridge the divide between biblical Christianity and the secular culture.
The mixed church has come about as an attempt to allow a Christian to live a reasonably peacefully life in a culture dominated by secular, humanistic, and relativistic values and behaviors. It is a mixture of biblical elements and secular elements (Rev. 3:14-22.) How much secularism is mixed in with biblical elements varies from Christian to Christian and church to church.

Let us face the reality that living a consistent biblical life in a non-Christian culture is difficult (1 Pet. 4:12-19.) American believers, for the most part, have not faced this for generations. It requires costly choices that many are not

willing to make today. For example, why would a Christian send their children to be educated by secular humanists who do not believe the fundamental truths of Christianity? Certainly if there were reasonable options they would take advantage of them. But private schools are expensive.
About 25 years ago the first wave of Christians began the costly move to home schooling. The culture opposed them.

The educational institutions and the employment opportunities were not accommodating. To choose this route was to be at odds with most everything. How would their children cope in the job market? How could they be successful in careers?

The great majority of Christians have left their children in the public, secular schools of America. They have accepted the mixing of their Christianity in the educational area with the secular influence and values of our culture. The cost of the alternatives is too great. This is precisely what the vast majority of our churches have done in many areas when faced with either accepting a mix of secular and biblical values or losing their members.

The world's music is now found in our churches. The world's opinions on marriage are now accepted in many churches. The world's sexual behavior is now condoned and defended in many mixed churches. Instead of maintaining biblical values and standards in our churches the mixed church has openly pursued a strategy of accepting the concepts and behaviors of the culture. *"We must win them to Christ by making them comfortable in our churches"* is the argument for mixing. It has been a devastating strategy, ruining the holiness, purity, and usefulness of our churches to be light in a dark day.
Evangelism under Fire

By almost any metric, the churches in our nation are much less evangelistic today than they were in the recent past. Today, we are reaching non-Christians only half as effectively as we were 50 years ago. The trend is disturbing.

We certainly see the pattern in the early church where "every day the Lord added to them those who were being saved" (Acts 2:47). Thom S. Rainer, the president and CEO of LifeWay Christian Resources, conducted a unscientific Twitter poll to see what church leaders and church members thought of this trend. The specific question was: "Why do you think many churches aren't as evangelistic as they once were?" The responses arrived quickly and in great numbers, the response was highly informative.

Here are the top ten responses listed:

- Christians have no sense of urgency to reach lost people.
- Our churches have an ineffective evangelistic strategy of "you come" rather than "we go."
- Many church members think that evangelism is the role of the pastor and paid staff.
- Church membership today is more about getting the members' needs met rather than reaching the lost.
- Church members are in a retreat mode as culture becomes more worldly and unbiblical.
- Many church members don't really believe that Christ is the only way to salvation.
- Our churches are no longer houses of prayer equipped to reach the lost.
- The average professed Christian does not attend prayer or Bible study during the week on a regular bases.
- Churches have lost their focus on making disciples who will thus be equipped and motivated to reach the

lost.
- Christians do not want to share the truth of the gospel for fear they will offend others. Political correctness is too commonplace even among Christians.
- Most churches have unregenerate members who have not received Christ themselves.

Today preaching and teaching has become soft and without power as many have reverted to motivational life coach messages in order to build houses but while failing to spiritually build the people. Recently a new television show on Fox Network came out called, "The Preachers." This was amazing in the fact that a secular network was going to have a talk show with preachers who actually pastored churches. The idea was that they would have normal everyday topics that didn't necessarily deal with a church setting. But once again we begin to see that biblical standards are no longer the norm even when you're a preacher on a secular network.

One particular show was about having an open marriage. A well-known actress and her husband came on the show to talk about how they enjoyed their open marriage. To my surprise not one of the preachers during the interview corrected this thinking and one in particular joked about being in an open marriage as he said, "But my wife didn't know it." One would have thought that he wouldn't have joked about that subject since he lost his wife to infidelity caused by him. Later at the end of the show one preacher did address the fact that this was not God's standard and that he disagreed with the actress views. However the preachers could have been more effective had they addressed the issue while she was sitting in front of them, and while millions were watching from home. What if some had turned the TV off before the end of the show to hear the corrected view?

On national secular television these appointed mouth pieces for the Kingdom of God did not seize the opportunity to let this Actress know, God's biblical standard of marriage, rather they chose to joke around with her. The following show didn't get any better as their next guest was an open transsexual celebrity by the name of Rupaul, whom they congratulated on his success in music and TV. This is a sad example of how far from God and desensitized the Church and our society has become.

Desensitization can be well-illustrated through a story I heard years ago. Eskimos in the barren North often kill wolves by taking a razor sharp knife and dipping it in blood. They allow the blood to freeze to the blade. Then they bury the handle of the knife in the snow with the blade exposed. As the wolf begins to lick the blade, his tongue becomes numb and desensitized due to the cold. As he continues, his tongue begins to bleed, and he licks even faster—unaware that he is consuming his own blood and slowly killing himself.

Within time, the Eskimos return and bring the dead animal home. In the same way, the enemy numbs us through compromise by what we allow into our mind. Within time, we, like the wolves, don't see that we are dying—dying spiritually.

The enemy desensitizes us until we are numb to the things of God ... until conviction fades. For example, why do so many enjoy movies and programs that glorify illicit sex, witchcraft, the occult, extreme violence, vampires and child sacrifice? Incredibly, what God calls an abomination is today's entertainment. Busy schedules and humanistic thinking has led us to have no time for prayer and devotion, but plenty of time for entertainment. Many will now forsake church service or duties in order to enjoy entertainment with friends and family.

Today's Church runs from speaking the truth for the fear of losing attendance and finances. Some become puppets of the big givers in their congregations. So the Word of God is soft and the standards of God are diluted. We say things like, "God doesn't move that way anymore," or "Can we just love everyone and forget the issues." There is a scripture in John 8:32 that says, "And you shall know the truth and the truth shall set you free." It's time for the Church of God to get back to the business of God, which is to tell a dying and sinful world that they need a living and loving Savior.

The Church must get back to the days where the presence of God is more important than crowds and popularity. Author John Bevere said, "We have replaced presence with atmosphere, but only presence transforms." Music ministries must understand we are not in concert on Sunday but rather we are at war in the spirit. When you worship healing and deliverance should take place. The scales should fall off the eyes of people who have lost their vision. Our message must be a message of change and transformation. We must awake out of our slumber and sound the alarm of the resurrection power of Jesus Christ.

"THE FRUSTRATING THING IS THOSE WHO ARE ATTACKING RELIGION CLAIM THEY ARE DOING IT IN THE NAME OF TOLERANCE, FREEDOM AND OPEN- MINDEDNESS. BUT ISN'T THE REAL TRUTH THAT THEY ARE INTOLERANT OF RELIGION? THEY REFUSE TO TOLERATE ITS IMPORTANCE IN OUR LIVES."

– PRESIDENT *Ronald Reagan*

CHAPTER 3
War on Christianity

Never in a time in my life have I seen the attack on Christianity so deliberate and calculated. There is also disrespect for the Word of God as the guiding path for which we, the Church, base our decisions and direction on.. In 2 Timothy Chapter 4:2-5 (GW) the Bible tells us of this season when people would not want the Word. *"Be ready to spread the word whether or not the time is right. Point out errors, warn people, and encourage them. Be very patient when you teach. A time will come when people will not listen to accurate teachings. Instead, they will follow their own desires and surround themselves with teachers who tell them what they want to hear. People will refuse to listen to the truth and turn to myths."*

Timothy was saying there will come a time when people will have no stomach for solid biblical teaching, but will chose to fill up on spiritual junk food. They will be intrigued by catchy opinions and turn their back on truth. But you must keep the message alive and stay focused on what you are doing as a servant of the living God. The Apostle Paul warned that in the last days there would be plenty of teachers who would refuse to teach sound doctrine. Jude also warned of those who would slip into leadership positions and turn God's grace into a license to sin. Today we see evidence of this everywhere, not only in churches, but also in our government and public school system.

Christianity is a religion of instruction. Where there is no solid biblical instruction, the Christian system can neither commence nor continue. Knowledge is the prerequisite to identifying with the faith of the gospel. Jesus declared that favor with God must involve instruction, reception, comprehension, and commitment (John 6:45).

The Church today is facing a time of great crisis. We have those among us who have pathetically low regard for the concept of Bible inspiration/authority. Many people are very fuzzy on what constitutes a Christian. A number of prominent personalities contend that the church must jazz-up its services to appeal to an entertainment-oriented culture. Basic truth has been thrown to the wind. The Church has on its hands a new generation of preachers who have matriculated through some of our schools and denominational seminaries, but who do not understand the most elementary matters about the role of the gospel preacher. They are experts in everything but the Word of God.

Our homes are void of biblical instruction. Domestic lives are so crowded –both mom and dad working, children involved in school, sports, etc. – that virtually all religious instruction has been left up to the Church. Most congregations are suffering serious attendance problems. Only a fraction of the local church attends Sunday or mid-week meetings. Aside from the Sunday morning assembly, only a skeleton crew will attend the services of a gospel service. Also disturbing is the way in which most children of God regard the services of the church. They will neglect the assemblies for trivial circumstances—even with the leaders, this is a common occurrence.

The crisis we face is real and deadly. Unless there is a revival of interest among leaders, unless there is a rekindling of passion for the cause of Christ within the Church, we are headed for rough times. Jesus spent three and half years of His life trying to build passion in the disciples for Kingdom work. He wanted them to desire the Word of God for their life and for the lives that they would touch. He wanted them to value the Word of God. When Jesus asked Peter who He was and Peter responded with the right answer, Jesus said, "Now I can build my Church, and the gates of hell will not prevail against it." He was simply saying to Peter, "Now that I know that you know the Word we can build the Father's Church.

If we are to build God's Church we will need the power of the Word of God. The word of God guarantees our success and stability as long as we follow the instructions given to Joshua. God told Joshua in Chapter 1 verse 8 it says, "Never stop reciting these teachings. You must think about them night and day so that you will faithfully do everything written in them. Only then will you prosper and succeed." Printed on our currency are the words, "In God We Trust." I believe when we get back to honoring God and His Word our nation will be prosperous and successful again.

"FOR ALL AUTHORITY COMES FROM GOD, AND THOSE IN POSITIONS OF AUTHORITY HAVE BEEN PLACED THERE BY GOD. SO ANYONE WHO REBELS AGAINST AUTHORITY IS REBELLING AGAINST WHAT GOD HAS INSTITUTED."

Romans 13:1-2 NLT

CHAPTER 4
Authority Under fire

Hebrews 13:17 (NLT) "Obey your spiritual leaders, and do what they say. Their work is to watch over your souls, and they are accountable to God. Give them reason to do this with joy and not with sorrow. That would certainly not be for your benefit." The modern church has largely turned away from the biblical pattern of pastoral respect and authority. The Israel of God is always severely tempted to "spoil the Egyptians" in an unlawful manner. Ever since the early Apologists, right through the Scholastic era, and up to this day, the church has largely departed from her governmental pattern shown to her in the Scripture. Even during the Reformation, for all its conquests and attainments, the area of church government was not tackled as radically as one would wish. By this I mean that the pastor was looked up to beyond scriptural warrant, or else he was merely a figure-head, with a name to lead but in actual fact the leadership was in somebody else's hands.

Especially in denominational churches, the type I grew up in, the pastor was expected to preach, but keep a safe distance from the congregation. The Church was usually under the control of trustees and deacons who hired and fired. The preacher was treated as a mere hired hand spokesman. Lastly, when it came to private counseling, his (biblical) admonition was hardly appreciated. The wayward Christian looked doubtfully at him as if to protest, "What right have you to intrude into my private affairs?"

The biblical pattern for the elder (pastor) is of a morally upright man, laboring among the people, and yet having oversight over them in the Lord. But I find from experience that though he is dedicated to his ministry, oftentimes the congregation accords him lip-honor, calling him "Pastor, Pastor," but is hardly willing to follow his doctrine (even the doctrines of grace) and his example.

It follows that the church in general is anemic: everybody wants to do what is right in his own eyes. The lessons of history are brushed aside as unimportant. Pragmatism is the order of the day: we will accept to do this and that if it works, if it renders certain results. The democratic ideal, taken from the Greeks, and so popular in our politics assumed to be necessarily the best form of government is borrowed and imported into the church. The people expect to have their individual vote. I do not see this in Scripture.

Decision-making is not in the hands of the people, but the people are brought up to think that they manage their own affairs, and are never confronted with the biblical ideal. Many good Pastors have been burnt out because they feel they can't pastor their congregations. They are under congregational control and can't do what they feel God has called them to do. I too faced a similar situation in my ministry.

Christ gives gifts to men (pastors to lead), but these gifts are unappreciated. In saying all this I do not mean that the eldership is to be tyrannical and unheeding to the cry of the congregation; what I mean is that the eldership should strive to get their orders from Christ through the Scripture and not to be dictated to by the congregation. But this is hardly to be seen today with any consistency.

Out of Control Society

Even the respect for authority, in our society and public school systems, are almost obsolete. Growing up I was taught to respect the teacher's authority and many times if you got into trouble with the teacher you would be in trouble once you got home. Also back then you would get immediate discipline from the teacher or administrator by being paddled. Many groups rose to oppose this form of discipline calling it child abuse. But for many of us it kept us on the straight and narrow. Today students have more rights than the adults, and they know it. It prevents the adult from having any control. Students are more violent and out of control than ever before. Even school Resource Officers, which are regular police officers, can't even get the respect that should be given.

When I worked in the public school system, I saw daily how it only took one student, who did not understand nor respect authority, to cause a teacher to lose control of their entire class. Resource Officers would be called to the classroom and would kindly ask the disruptive student to step outside so that they could speak with them privately. But because they did not respect the authority of the badge or the adult, they would not move as a stance of defiance. In many cases they would begin a verbal confrontation with the adult. Of course things didn't go well and the student would be removed by the officer, sometimes by force.

Today we see these same incidences taking place with the recent shootings by police officers. And because of a few bad officers or cell phones that only capture the last few moments of a situation, we now have escalated into an era of non-respect for authority. As a result we have fallen into a war with police officers and the African American community. For several months it seemed like a young black male was dying at the hands of police officers senselessly. Then we began to see the attack on police officers as they were gunned down in Dallas and other cities.

Our nation is in great need of reconciliation and healing. Many have lost faith in leaders in the Church, the community and in our government. We are in need of great leaders who can lead with the conviction of God in their hearts. We need Christians in politics that will govern with the mind of righteousness. And we need leaders in the Church who will get out of their comfort zone and lead a dying and confused generation back to God.

"When the righteous increase, the people rejoice, But when a wicked man rules, people groan."-Proverbs 29:2 (NASB)

"THEREFORE, SAY TO THE PEOPLE, 'THIS IS WHAT THE LORD OF HEAVEN'S ARMIES SAYS: RETURN TO ME, AND I WILL RETURN TO YOU, SAYS THE LORD OF HEAVEN'S ARMIES."

Zechariah 1:3 NLT

CHAPTER 5
Morality in Decline

America has plummeted from righteous living, prosperity and success in the last quarter century. America's moral decline rapidly accelerated following one event – the U.S. Supreme Court's removal of prayer from our nation's schools. On June 25, 1962, 39 million students were forbidden to do what they and their predecessors had been doing since the founding of our nation – publicly calling upon the name of the Lord at the beginning of each school day.

The New York school children who prompted the Engel vs. Vitale ruling had simply prayed: "Almighty God, we acknowledge our dependence on Thee and beg Thy blessing over us, our parents, our teachers and our nation." America has experienced radical decline in each of the four areas which the children's prayer touched upon: youth, family, education, national life.

Minor recovery had occurred during the 1980's when the election of President Reagan brought forth a renewed emphasis on "traditional" values. The removal of prayer from our schools was a violation of the third commandment which commands us "not to take the name of the Lord in vain." By the judicial act of forbidding invocation, the Court audaciously elevated a secularized system of education beyond the authority, reach and blessing of God Himself. Worse than taking the Lord's sacred name in vain is treating it with contempt, denying it rightful place and stripping it from public use and even from the lips of children. Jesus' own expressed desire, "Let the little children come to me, and do not forbid them" was also violated by these judges, many of whom were raised in Christian homes.

But there was actually a gross violation of the third commandment by the U.S. Supreme Court a year earlier. A ruling in 1961, I believe, paved the way for stripping the Lord's name from our children's lips. In Torcaso vs. Watkins, the court overruled a provision of the Maryland Constitution which made "a declaration of belief in the existence of God" mandatory for holding public office.

Roy R. Torcaso, a Maryland resident and an avowed atheist, was refused a notary public commission when he would not subscribe to the required oath. His case was brought before the U.S. Supreme Court. The Court ruled to sanction atheism and overruled the Maryland Constitution.
The effect of this ruling is not just to eat away at the sacredness of the name of God, but to eliminate the sacredness and thereby the substance of the oath itself. With solemn oaths and binding contracts between individuals removed, the state eventually sits where God ought, and only the state's cause is held valid. There is no longer an absolute and just legal basis for judging "between a man and his brother," much less a man and his neighbor (Deuteronomy 1:16-17). All affairs of life become subject to state, rather than individual control.

There is an organized attack reaching into high places is under way to remove the third commandment from legal standing in the United States and throughout the world." The World Court, for example, presumably the new fountain of justice, or a prototype of the socialist dream of world government, has no provision for taking the name of God' – no oath or covenant."

Jesus' teaching on oath-taking and covenant is recorded in Matthew 5:33-37, "You have also heard that our ancestors were told, 'You must not break your vows; you must carry out the vows you make to the Lord." But I say, do not make any vows! Do not say, 'By heaven!' because heaven is God's throne. And do not say, 'By the earth!' because the earth is his footstool. And do not say, 'By Jerusalem!' for Jerusalem is the city of the great King. Do not even say, 'By my head!' for you can't turn one hair white or black. Just say a simple, 'Yes, I will,' or 'No, I won't.' Anything beyond this is from the evil one. While often misinterpreted, this is actually a strong affirmation of the third commandment and a clear warning that "the Lord will not hold him guiltless who takes His name in vain."

SPIRITUAL LEAKAGE

The "evangelical prophet," Oswald Chambers (1874 – 1917), saw that the empty promises made by so many Christians actually result in great "spiritual leakage." He admonished his followers: "Always beware of vowing, it is a risky thing. If you promise to do a thing and don't do it, it means the weakening of your moral nature. We are all so unaware in the way we promise and don't perform and never realize that it is sapping our moral energy."

Think then, what happens to a nation rife with perjury, broken marriage covenants, unforgiveness, cults with demonic covenants, extortion, bribery, libel, slander, profanity, hypocrisy, idle talk, and lawsuits initiated solely for revenge and personal gain. We are living witnesses that truly the Lord does not hold such a nation guiltless. Regardless of how the U.S. Supreme Court has ruled, we must each realize that God's laws are not watered down to suit anyone; if God did that He would cease to be God.

Most people tend to believe that we can "fix this country" by getting the right politicians into power or by implementing certain economic or social reforms. But the reality of the matter is that our problems go far deeper than that. A moral collapse is eating away at the foundations of our society like cancer. If it continues to go unchecked, it will inevitably destroy America and the Church. Unfortunately, fixing moral decay is far more difficult than switching out political parties, because it is in the hearts of hundreds of millions of individual Americans. And most people don't want to hear anything about a "moral collapse", because most people like to think that the United States is setting a "good example" for the rest of the planet. But as you will see below, that is not the case at all. And if we are honest with ourselves, we see the evidence of this moral collapse all around us every day. Just consider a few of the news stories that we have seen recently…

What would cause a high school kid to take two kitchen knives and go on a stabbing rampage through his school?

What would cause a topless woman to ransack a McDonald's in St. Petersburg, Florida?

What would cause two 18-year-old boys to beat a 30-year-old mentally-disabled man to death with a baseball bat just so they could get his Xbox?

What would cause a new father to put his 6-week-old daughter in a freezer to keep her from crying?

What would cause a young mother to kill her daughter and bury her just so she can go out and party?

What would cause a man to walk into a night club and kill 49 people and wound 50 people in Orlando?

A lot of people, including the media, regard those kinds of stories as "isolated incidents", but as you will see below, they are actually representative of a much larger trend. As a society, we are decaying from the inside out, and we need to start facing the truth if we are ever going to get this turned around. The following are 20 facts about the moral collapse of America that are almost too crazy to believe…

1. Every single year, there are 20 million new STD cases in America, which has the highest STD infection rate in the entire industrialized world.

2. The United States has the highest teen pregnancy rate in the entire industrialized world.

3. It has been estimated that 89 percent of all pornography is produced in the United States.

4. The number of American babies killed by abortion each year is roughly equal to the number of U.S. military deaths that have occurred in all of the wars that the United States has ever been involved in combined.

5. Approximately 3,000 Americans lost their lives as a result of the destruction of the World Trade Center towers on 9/11. Every single day, more than 3,000 American babies are killed by abortion

6. Most women that get abortions in the United States claim to be Christian. Protestant women get 42 percent of all abortions and Catholic women get 27

percent of all abortions.

7. Approximately 52 percent of all African-American pregnancies now end in abortion.

8. One very shocking study found that 86 percent of all abortions are done for the sake of convenience.

9. An all-time high 59 percent of all Americans believe that the traditional definition of marriage needs to be changed.

10. The number of sexual assaults in the U.S. military is at an all-time high, and the majority of them are male on male incidents. During 2012, more than 85,000 military veterans were formally treated for sexual abuse that they suffered while serving in the U.S. military.

11. America has the highest incarceration rate and the largest total prison population in the entire world by a wide margin.

12. Americans spend more than 280 billion dollars on prescription drugs each year.

13. Right now, there are 70 million Americans that are on mind-altering drugs of one form or another.

14. In the United States today, prescription painkillers kills more Americans than heroin and cocaine combined.

15. Corruption is rampant throughout our society. In fact, America leads the world in money given to fake charities.

16. One study discovered that 88 percent of all Americans from age 8 to age 18 play video games, and that approximately four times as many boys are addicted to video games as girls are.

17. The number of Americans with no religious affiliation has grown by 25 percent over the past five years.

18. 73 percent of the religiously unaffiliated support gay marriage and 72 percent of the religiously unaffiliated support legalized abortion, and now make up 24 percent of all registered voters "who are Democrats or lean Democratic".

19. A study conducted by the Barna Group discovered that nearly 60 percent of all Christians from 15 years of age to 29 years of age are no longer actively involved in any church.

20. It is being projected that the percentage of Americans attending church in 2050 will be about half of what it is today.

As you can see it has become very clear that the decline of morality leads to a decline of respect for life and God. I believe that the book of Zechariah sums it all up.

"Therefore tell the people; this is what the Lord Almighty says; "Return to me declares the Lord Almighty and I will return to you." Zechariah 1:3 (NLT) If we are to be a great Christian nation again we must turn back to God.

"AND HE ANSWERED AND SAID, "HAVE YOU NOT READ THAT HE WHO CREATED THEM FROM THE BEGINNING MADE THEM MALE AND FEMALE, AND SAID, 'FOR THIS REASON A MAN SHALL LEAVE HIS FATHER AND MOTHER AND BE JOINED TO HIS WIFE, AND THE TWO SHALL BECOME ONE FLESH'? SO THEY ARE NO LONGER TWO, BUT ONE FLESH. WHAT THEREFORE GOD HAS JOINED TOGETHER, LET NO MAN SEPARATE."

Matthew 19:4-6 NASB

CHAPTER 6
Family and Marriage Redefined

Marriage is one of life's biggest and special unions. It's a time when two lives join as one – two people who possibly come from different backgrounds join to become one new family unit. It may be the first time you ever considered something old, something new, something borrowed, and something blue! The wedding day can be a rollercoaster of sorts, going from times of extreme happiness to the point of tears. But most importantly marriage is the culmination of God's plan for a man and a woman.

One of my favorite authors is Max Lucado, who said, "God created marriage. No government subcommittee envisioned it. No social organization developed it. Marriage was conceived and born in the mind of God."

God Himself emphasizes that right behavior on the part of His people in marriage is an important aspect of our responsibility to keep the covenant. He emphasizes this when He made marriage the outstanding symbol of His covenant with us. Throughout the Old Testament, for example, Jeremiah 3 and Ezekiel 16, God teaches that He is married to Israel/Judah. In Isaiah 54:5-6, God is called Judah's husband, and Judah is called Jehovah's wife. In the New Testament, Ephesians 5:22, teaches that God is the husband of the church in Jesus Christ. God's spiritual marriage to the church is the covenant.

If marriage is nothing less than the symbol of the covenant, our behavior in marriage is certainly an important part of our keeping the covenant. We are called to show the truth of the covenant in our marriage. God emphasizes the importance of our behavior in marriage.

This is the teaching of Ephesians 5:22. The Christian husband is commanded to behave towards his wife as Christ behaves towards the church, and the Christian wife is commanded to behave towards her husband as the church behaves towards Christ.

The New Normal?

The comparison implies that the covenant of God in Christ—the real and everlasting marriage—must be evident in our marriage. So closely are covenant and marriage connected in the lives of most of us. God's design for marriage is clear in His creation ordinance (Genesis 2:18-25). If humanity chooses to ignore that ordinance, the results are devastating. We are now seeing those results unfold with the new normal in family diversity and the increasing practice of cohabitation, which does not produce healthy marriages for the future. The generation today does not promote traditional marriage.

Below are five staggering statistics that show the decline in marriage.

- The marriage rate in the United States has fallen to an all-time low. Right now it is sitting at a yearly rate of 6.8 marriages per 1000 people.

- America has the highest percentage of one person households on the entire planet. Approximately one out of every three children in the United States lives in a home without a father.

- According to the Pew Research Center, only 51 percent of all American adults are currently married. Back in 1960, 72 percent of all adults in the United States were married.

- In the USA more than 50% of all couples "move in together" before they get married. As a result more children are being born to cohabiting couples.

- America has the highest divorce rate in the world by a good margin.

Your marriage is not being attacked because you two don't understand each other. It's being attacked because there is a covenant attached to it and the enemy wants it. The marriage covenant as God has ordained it is under severe attack. There is even an agenda to present a new norm through political means. Some want to create a world where the words male or female, husband or wife do not exist, and where marrying the same sex or multiple people is acceptable.

Redefining what God Defined

June 26th, 2015 was a day I'll never forget. I was home watching the televised funeral service of the Charleston church massacre, where nine people had been assassinated by a gunman, when suddenly the broadcast was interrupted to announce that gay marriage, had now become legal in all 50 states by the United States Supreme Court. This was shocking and I couldn't help but think of how the Church fell asleep on this and ignored it like they did with prayer in school.

No one could have ever imagined that the United States Supreme Court would ever redefine what God had already defined. What was respected since the very foundation of the earth was now changed by one vote of just nine people. I immediately filed an online petition called the Pastors Protection Act of Florida. I really didn't think that it would go anywhere and I certainly had not been engaged in politics to that degree. But to my surprise within two weeks I had gathered 24,000 signatures across the State of Florida. I was then introduced to some state elected officials who began drafting a bill to present to the next legislative session.

For nine months I and 25 other pastors across the state, along with the Christian Family Coalition of Florida, fought through six committees. Many LGBT people, including gay ministers, came out in opposition to our bill. It was amazing to see how well organized and determined the LGBT was to get their ideology recognized. It allowed me to see that we as the Church could no longer sit in our padded pews and beautifully crafted buildings while our religious rights were being trampled on. I also saw how wicked our elected officials had gotten, as committee by committee, many of them came in support of the LBGT agenda.

It was at this moment I came to a conclusion that the Church had missed the boat. Somehow we had been convinced to stay in our sanctuaries, conduct our nice conferences, focus on church growth and stay out of politics. You see the LGBT figured it out, that the real power was in policy change. So as we were exiting politics they were entering, and their mission was generational change.

I quickly learned that they had used the civil rights

movement of African Americans as their agenda to fight for equal rights. I, as an African American, was appalled at this notion, as our fight was about "skin" and theirs was about "sin." We didn't have a right to choose our skin color but they certainly believed they had a right to choose to live a lifestyle that was contrary to God's standards. Our ancestors didn't choose to come to America stacked on ships, but the LGBT community did choose to come out of the closet.

A Church Divided

Fighting for this bill also allowed me to see that the Church was divided.

Several pastors were against our bill and even spoke on behalf of the LGBT community, stating that our bill was discriminatory and that God was all about love. I certainly believe that God is about love but He never condoned sin. Traveling to the State Capital for those nine months made me realize more and more that it was time for Christians to get back into the political arena.

There were several amendments that were presented that would have been very dangerous to the Church. One in particular was to re-define the definition of a religious institution and the other was to designate the Church as a public accommodation. Both attempts failed in subcommittee vote, but had they passed, the church would have been forced to offer its facilities to LGBT groups, including choosing their bathroom of choice.

We were a small army compared to the bus loads of LGBT individuals that were brought in for every hearing, but after nine months and six subcommittee meetings, a State House and State Senate vote, we were able to get the Pastor

Protection Bill passed into Law! I was even honored to be made the Pastor of the Day and was given the opportunity to pray over the State House legislators before they made the vote.

Gender Identity Crisis

Now we are in one of the most heated political seasons this nation has ever faced.

The safety of our children is now in question at our public schools and institutions. As I am writing this book just a few months ago the President of the United States, the Secretary of Education and the Department of Justice issued a national directive to all school districts in the nation to allow transgender students to use whatever bathroom that they identify with. I was so stunned and upset I immediately filed a petition online on *change.org* called "Say No to Transgender Restrooms Florida" and within the first week over 18,000 people had signed it.

Sadly, news media and radio shows were reporting to the public that the LGBT community was being unfairly discriminated against. The truth was that people were simply concerned about the safety and security of women and children. The administration's 25-page booklet of proposed policies approvingly cites a Colorado school district, which says teachers must embrace "the goals of maximizing the [transgender] student's social integration and equal opportunity to participate in overnight activity and athletic trips, ensuring the [transgender] student's safety and comfort, and minimizing stigmatization of the [again, transgender] student."

The President's adopted hometown of Chicago is more insistent: "In no case should a transgender student be denied the right to participate in an overnight field trip because of the student's transgender status." So, any individual who says he is a member of the opposite sex (says he is a female) must be allowed to spend the night in the same room as members of the opposite biological sex for his "social integration" and "comfort."

Suppose a teenage boy discovers he is "transgender" just in time to spend the night in his girlfriend's hotel room? Or the hotel room of a girl who is decidedly not his girlfriend? He must be allowed to do so without a chaperone, unless there's an adult in every room. Don't forget, under civil rights law, there can be no disparate treatment. If transgender students are chaperoned but "other" girls aren't, that's profiling and could trigger a federal civil rights lawsuit from the social justice warriors.

So, your daughter may not know she will be spending the night with a boy until she gets to her hotel room. Unthinkable as this would be, it hardly scratches the surface. The administration makes it clear, "In this letter, the term *schools* refers to recipients of federal financial assistance at all educational levels, including school districts, colleges, and universities." All of this is being forced on the nation without one legislator voting to authorize it, or even a public debate to consult the views of the American people. If Christians don't speak up now we will lose an entire generation to a culture who no longer respects God or morality. We can't sit idle while marriage is being attacked in the courts, identity is being redefined and our children's safety is at risk. We need a generation whose heart is turned back to the Father. A generation who honors the covenant, that was established, before they were in their mother womb.

WISDOM IS THE PRINCIPAL THING; IN ALL THY GETTING GET AN UNDERSTANDING."

Proverbs 4:7 (NLT)

CHAPTER 7
War on Wisdom

There is a scripture in Jeremiah 6:10 that says, "To whom shall I speak and give warning that they may hear? Behold, their ears are closed and they cannot listen. Behold, the word of the Lord has become a reproach to them; they have no delight in it."Even in today's Christian Church the Word of God has become watered down. We have resulted to motivational life application messages. Our church environments have been redesigned into social atmospheres of convenience rather than atmospheres of change. The hyper grace teachings have infiltrated the wholeness of the gospel to the point that condemnation is confused with conviction. The Word of God was designed to transform and convict the reader to change. Truth is now the new terrorist that people don't want to deal with. I believe we are truly living in the last days, where the hearts of men are waxing cold, good is becoming evil and evil is becoming good.

We now have "self-help" Christianity where people feel they don't need a mentor of the word. Today statistics show only 7% of people who get saved stay saved after 10 years. The word coming from the pulpits today is too often weakening, rather than empowering, God's people. Have you ever heard the phrase "eye candy"? It's a popular term that describes what is pleasing and attractive to the sight. It's usually over the top, lots of lights, lots of spectacle, lots of fun and appealing to the eyes. Well, many of the messages coming from many pulpits in America could be classified as "ear candy."

Just as butter scotch taste sweet to the lips, these gospel messages are sweet to the ears. They cause the hearers to feel good and want more but never challenge them or cause them to spiritually mature. Too often, ear candy messages have become the main course of our spiritual diets rather than strong meat that strengthens our souls. But the Word of God clearly challenges us to help mature people through the power of God's Word. Ephesians 4:11-13, *"And He gave some as apostles, and some as prophets, and some as evangelists, and some as pastors and teachers, for the equipping of the [a]saints for the work of service, to the building up of the body of Christ; until we all attain to the unity of the faith, and of the knowledge of the Son of God."*

Deception in the Church

In New Testament times, the apostle Paul wrote to his young protégé, Timothy, warning him to do the things that will avoid the trend we are now seeing in the church:
"I charge you therefore before God and the Lord Jesus Christ, who will judge the living and the dead at His appearing and His kingdom: Preach the word! Be ready in season and out of season. Convince, rebuke, exhort, with all longsuffering and teaching. For the time will come when they will not endure sound doctrine, but according to their own desires, because they have itching ears, they will heap up for themselves teachers; and they will turn their ears away from the truth, and be turned aside to fables. But you be watchful in all things, endure afflictions, do the work of an evangelist, fulfill your ministry" (2 Tim. 4:1-5 NKJV).

The original Greek word translated fables here means "fiction" or "nonsense." Paul issued a similar warning to a group of believers in Corinth. False doctrine was being taught in this first-century church, threatening to weaken its spiritual foundation. The deception Paul warned about is rampant today in America and all over the World, and we are concerned for the Church of God.

We've all heard the adage that a spoonful of sugar helps the medicine go down. That may be true. But today, in the spiritual sense, there is no medicine coming behind the ear candy. The doctors of the Word, the clergy, are afraid to prescribe the medicine that was made available from heaven's pharmacy 2,000 years ago. They see the disease but are afraid to properly treat it for fear of offending or losing a crowd. They have become tolerant, soft and weak in the Word.

From God's perspective, the diagnosis and treatment have always been clear: Sin is the disease. The blood of Christ is the cure. Repentance is God's method for putting the two together. The devastating results of slipping away from proclaiming fundamental, doctrinal truths are already evident in our society. It is essential that we teach the whole counsel of God.

We must all feel the responsibility. We must carry the burden. We must share in the load if we are to successfully carry out our part of the Great Commission. Even now, we are watching churches all over America slip into this abyss. Pastors who were at one time filled with the Holy Spirit—who spoke in tongues and prayed for the sick—now won't permit the Spirit of God to move in their services. No more manifestations of the Spirit. No more encouraging prophecy. No more crying after God. Instead, they serve up silly short life messages with coffee and a donut.

What is happening? We're allowing the people to decide what to eat for their spiritual dinner. Rather than toiling to prepare some fresh bread from heaven and offering them a clean, cool cup of water from God's fountain, we are letting their desires determine the meals we serve. What parent would allow their children to decide the evening's menu? Their plates would be full of cookies, cake and candy!

We believe the devil's favorite time of the week here in America is Sunday morning. We don't think he minds seeing people go to church. In fact, we think he wants to get as many people to church as possible because he knows they'll hear a sugar-coated, lukewarm message.

They'll go to a 45-minute service in which the sermon is barely 20 minutes long. They have a "religious itch," and the pastor will scratch it by saying, "You're fine. Everything's wonderful. Everything's OK." Then they'll walk out feeling good about themselves. All the while, they're living in sin and thinking nothing of it.

The power of God's Word is derived from God Himself. God is omniscient, able to see into the hearts of men; therefore His Word is able to cut to the hearts of men and reveal their true nature, therefore how we react to the Word of God reveals our true character.

Hebrews 4:12 (AMP)............12For the Word that God speaks is alive and full of power [making it active, operative, energizing, and effective]; it is sharper than any two-edged sword, penetrating to the dividing line of the [a]breath of life (soul) and [the immortal] spirit, and of joints and marrow [of the deepest parts of our nature], exposing and sifting and analyzing and judging the very thoughts and purposes of the heart.

Attack of the WORD

Across our nation you can see the very beginnings of the attack on the Word of God. Recently a lay pastor in

Georgia, Dr. Eric Walsh was issued a legal demand by the State of Georgia to hand over his sermons, sermons notes and all pastoral documentation, including his bible. This demand for Dr. Eric Walsh's sermons, sermons notes and ministerial documentation is an alarming display of government intrusion into the sanctity of the church, pastor's study and pulpit," said Tony Perkins, Family Research Council president and himself an ordained pastor. The pulpit is to be governed only by the Word of God. Government scrutiny of speech in the pulpit is unconstitutional and unconscionable. The Family Research, led by Tony Perkins called for the State of Georgia to cease its hostility toward people of faith.

This isn't the first time we've witnessed the attack on the Word or hostility toward people of faith as the former mayor of Houston, the city's first openly lesbian mayor, issued subpoenas against pastors in Houston, Texas, seeking their sermons and notes dealing with homosexuality and gender identity. Mayor Parker went a step farther and threatened that those ministers who failed to comply could be held in contempt of court.

The pastors filed a motion in Harris County court to stop the subpoenas arguing they are "overbroad, unduly burdensome, harassing, and vexatious." This sparked national outrage by Christians across America. Houston City Hall was deluged with telephone calls, letters, emails – along with hundreds of Bibles and sermons. And more than 50,000 supporters signed a petition to stop the Mayors over reach of power.

Although the Mayor withdrew her subpoena under pressure, she was hell-bent on defending the Houston Equal Rights Ordinance – a piece of legislation that would in part give grown men who identify as women the right to use the restrooms of their choice. Today the Word of God is now the new terrorist and religion is seen as a hate group. We are truly in the last days where it says, *"They exchanged the truth about God for a lie, and worshiped and served created things rather than the Creator—who is forever."* (Romans 1:25)

The good news is we can turn this around, but we must repent and return back to God as a nation. 2 Chronicles 7:14 says, "If my people, which are called by my name, shall humble themselves, and pray, and seek my face, and turn from their wicked ways; then will I hear from heaven, and will forgive their sin, and will heal their land." But notice it says, "IF", which is always a notation of the condition of heart. We have to see that we need to change and turn from our wicked ways in order for God to heal this land. We just can't be satisfied with prayer vigils that don't result in the change of heart. God is calling His Church and His people to uphold the integrity of His Word. Will you be one of them?

The dumbing down of American education has begun. Apparently working your hardest to be the best you can be—and being recognized for the effort—is one lesson a North Carolina School Board no longer believes is worth teaching. High school valedictorians are on the verge of becoming a thing of the past in Wake County as school leaders cut down on what they call unhealthy competition among top-achieving students.

The Wake County School Board unanimously gave initial approval this year to a policy that would bar high school principals from naming valedictorians and salutatorians—titles which go to the two seniors with the highest grade-point averages—after 2018. Starting in 2019, high schools will begin using a new system that recognizes seniors with Latin titles such as *cum laude* if they have a weighted GPA of at least 3.75. School Board members said the change will allow students to take more of the courses they'd like rather than just the ones that will boost their GPA and class rank. School Board Chairman Tom Benton stated in an interview that he had heard from many schools that the competition had become very unhealthy. He believed that students were not collaborating with each other the way that they wanted them to. Benton felt that their choice of courses was being guided by their GPA and not their future education plans.

The new system would result in more seniors being recognized especially in schools where there could be 400 to 600 seniors. The only problem with this entire plan is that it eliminates the students' desire to achieve and be their best as there is no end goal. We are a nation built on competition and there is nothing wrong with it. This is the beginning of dumbing down education in America. This is what they do with trophies in little league and other sports teams; everyone gets a participation ribbon, so why bother to work hard to be the best you can?

In addition, Ivy League schools use valedictorian status as one of the criteria in deciding whom to accept. If you want to prevent your high school student from having a chance at an Ivy League school then this policy is great. Let's start with correcting the grading system that is hindering children from achieving. We have to teach that LIFE is a competition. JOBS are a competition. And striving for the best and challenging yourself is very healthy. Schools used to prepare students for life; unfortunately now they are only prepared to expect instant gratification and a safe room when anything offends them. They're not doing these kids any favors by filling their heads with the delusion that performance doesn't matter. Unfortunately it does matter in the real world, and these kids are going to get hit by life like a speeding bus.

There have been valedictorians and salutatorians since the advent of the graduation ceremony, and somehow, we all miraculously survived. You know why? For one thing, the vast majority of us weren't obsessed with our GPA's. We *cared* about them, of course, but it wasn't the only thing that mattered. We did our best, knowing that there was always going to be somebody better at one subject or another.

The only thing this policy will accomplish is to minimize the accomplishments of the true valedictorian and salutatorian in each class. Now we have a new "war"—a war on intelligence. We dumb down education and turn schools into propaganda institutions, promote sexual deviancy, Islam, and mediocrity and suppress the concepts of morality, excellence, and motivation.

As a former high school educator for over 12 years, a part of me understands the logic of this. I have seen kids work hard for their GPA and others cheat their way to the top. I also understand that we must honor the ones who have achieved the rank of valedictorian and salutatorian. The most disturbing thing I am feeling about this new policy is it seems to not reward excellence and it may be more of a leveling move. I find this, another example of socialistic conformity, instead of individualist excellence.

All of the top companies are trying to loosen immigration requirements so they can attract foreign workers to high tech jobs because there are not enough qualified Americans to fill the jobs. Today a degree in psychology will get you nothing but a low paying retail job. There is not a school of engineering in this country where Americans make up the majority. We should be doing everything we can to increase competition, not eliminate it.

There is nothing wrong with a little competition that requires you to put forth your best effort. For the scriptures declare in, 1 Corinthians 9:24-25 that, "not everyone who competes will get the prize, but run like you will." Let's teach our children the value of striving for something and that they can do all things through Christ that gives them the strength.

"SINCE WE OUGHT TO BE NO LESS PERSUADED THAT THE PROPITIOUS SMILES OF HEAVEN, CAN NEVER BE EXPECTED ON A NATION THAT DISREGARDS THE ETERNAL RULES OF ORDER AND RIGHT, WHICH HEAVEN ITSELF HAS ORDAINED."

PRESIDENT *George Washington*

CHAPTER 8
Renewing Our First Love

In his first inaugural address President George Washington made it clear that no nation can expect to be blessed by God (propitious smiles of Heaven) if they turn away from Him. He knew if a nation forgets God she will lose the blessing that God has given her. Representing the nation, Washington made a promise that the United States of America would follow God. But if she ever broke her promise then she would lose God's blessing and protection. God would keep His promise. He always kept His promises. Only one question remained: Would the United States of America keep hers?

America became by far one of the greatest super powers on planet earth. Known for its vast wealth, economic power, military strength, and political influence, America has been the leader of the modern free world. Our nation's forefathers strongly believed they were called into a new promised land for the purpose of establishing a New Israel, a model of the Kingdom of God – living proof that in God's economy people from every station of life could live in peace and prosperity together.

They believed God's promises to Israel, barring those that were most specific to the Jews, were also pledged to any nation that would enter into a covenant relationship with Him. Basing our nation's principles of law and government on the Judeo-Christian ethic, they sought to initiate and admonish succeeding generations to maintain a covenant relationship with the Lord like the one made with the Israelites in Deuteronomy Chapter 28.

No one better set the ground work and expressed America's destiny as an exceptional nation state than John Winthrop, who along with his fellow Puritans in 1630 traveled across the Atlantic to build "a city upon a hill." Winthrop stated in his speech aboard the Arbella: *"When God gives a commission, He looks to have it strictly observed in every article...Thus stands the cause between God and us." We are entered into covenant with Him for His work. We have taken out a commission. The Lord hath given us leave to draw our own articles. We have professed to enterprise these and those accounts, upon these and those ends.*

We have sought Him for favor and blessing. Now if the Lord shall please to hear us, and bring us in peace to the place we desire, then, has He ratified the covenant and sealed our commission, and will expect a strict performance of the articles contained in it."

Words to this effect were mentioned over and again by America's founding fathers and other leadership through the decades. If we take a look at the book of Deuteronomy Chapter 28, it gives us a clear picture of why America has experienced unprecedented blessings from God, because we honored Him:

1. You will be blessed in the city and you will be blessed in the country (v.3) *Example:* America's prosperity is known throughout the world.

2. The fruit of your womb will be blessed (v.4) *Example:* Generations will be strong and set apart.

3. The crops of your land will be blessed (v.4)

Example: America is the breadbasket of the world.

4. Your calves and your lambs will be blessed (v.4) *Example:* Fertile grazing land, producing healthy and bountiful herds.

5. Your basket and kneading trough will be blessed (v.5) *Example:* Robust and prosperous business, trade, and production.

6. You will be blessed when you go in and when you go out (v.6) *Example:* Freedom of travel.

7. Your enemies will be defeated (v.7) *Example*: America is the greatest and strongest military power and has never lost a war until Vietnam.

8. The Lord will send a blessing on your barn and everything you do (v.8) *Example*: Abundant prosperity.

9. The Lord will bless you in the land He is giving you (v.8) *Example:* Health and wealth.

10. The Lord will establish you as a holy people (v.9) *Example:* America was viewed as a Christian nation.

11. Then all the peoples on the earth will see that you are called by the name of the Lord and they will fear you (v.10). *Example:* America's prominence throughout the world.

12. The Lord will grant you abundant prosperity (v.11). *Example:* America has the highest living standard in the world.

13. The Lord will open the heavens, the storehouse of His bounty, to send rain on your land in season and to bless all the work of your hands (v.12) *Example:* Favorable climates producing bountiful harvests.

14. You will lend to many nations but will borrow from none (v.12) *Example:* America never accumulated debt until the early 60s.

15. The Lord will make you head and not the tail…You will always be at the top, never at the bottom (v.13) *Example*: America has always been a top nation among other nations.

Just as God abundantly blessed Israel and used that nation as an example to the world in ancient days, in more modern times He exalted America to show the world how He rewards those nations that devote themselves to Him.

Let us be mindful of the warning in Deuteronomy 28:15: *"However, if you do not obey the Lord your God and do not carefully follow all His commands and decrees I am giving you today, all these curses will come upon you and overtake you…"*

Think of it. When a nation breaks its covenant with God, as America has characteristically been doing in recent years, the blessings start to turn into curses. Some of these curses we already see taking place in the last two decades such as:

1. Your basket and kneading trough will be cursed (v.17) *Example*: Failing industry.

2. The fruit of your womb will be cursed (v.18) *Example:* The birth of children, which are a blessing and the future of a nation are greatly

limited in number by abortion and in various ways impaired via serious diseases, disasters, and death.

3. The crops of your lands will be cursed (v.18:38-40) *Example*: Wildfires, floods, various natural catastrophes that destroy the heartland.

4. Your calves and lambs will be cursed (v.18) *Example*: Falling prices, rising costs, and the failure of farm-life.

5. Confusion surrounding everything you do (v.20) *Example:* A serious lack of direction about what to do to effectively address the nation's problems. Even both major political parties have no answers.

6. The Lord will plague you with...the Lord will strike you with wasting disease (v.21-22) *Example*: Hundreds of STDs, HIV and AIDS, and many other illnesses that are fatal- for which no known remedy can seem to be found.

7. Scorching heat and drought (v.22) *Example*: So-called global warming. Right now we are facing the hottest summer on record in the USA.

8. The Lord will turn the rain into dust...it will (then) come down, until you are destroyed (v.24). *Example*: Hurricanes, tornadoes, floods, and unusual violent weather patterns are taking place across the country like never before.

9. The Lord will cause you to be defeated on the battlefields (v.25). *Example:* Vietnam. A general inability to finally resolve a serious threat through a necessary military action.

10. The Lord will afflict you with tumors and festering sores (v.27) *Example*: Cancer taking the lives of thousands, with no cure actually in sight. AIDS, etc.

11. The Lord will afflict you with madness...confusion of mind (v. 28) *Example:* A rise in mental disorders, depression, and anxiety.

12. You will be oppressed and robbed (v.29) *Example:* An explosion in political corruption and crime is running rampant in our nation today.

13. You will be pledged to be married...but another will take her (v.30) *Example:* The breakdown of marriage and the rise of infidelity are now being showcased on television shows as the new norm.

14. The alien who lives among you will rise above you higher and higher (v.43) *Example:* Serious immigration issues that put citizens of the nation at a disadvantage. More immigrants are entering the United States at an alarming rate from various nations.

15. He will lend to you but you will not lend to him (v.44) *Example:* The country has become a debtor nation and the national debt is out of control in the trillions. China now holds America's debt.

These judgments are not meant to be applicable in every individual case, but they are meant to be seen collectively as curses upon the nation for its disobedience. Could there be any reasonable question America has abandoned its covenant with God? Though our beloved country has not experienced a final judgment, it is obviously already under judgment.

God help us. If the church doesn't repent of its own wickedness, and, if there is no great spiritual awakening, resulting in our nation renewing its covenant with God, then as a nation we are ultimately doomed. Puritan leader John Winthrop said, *"The eyes of all people are upon us. So that if we shall deal falsely with our God in this work we have undertaken, and so cause God to withdraw His present help from us, we shall be made a story and a byword through the world."*

Making America Great Again?

This year as I write this book we are in the most vicious election season that we have ever experienced in our history. Both candidates no doubt have circumstances that cause eyebrows and questions to be raised. But one candidate is running on the slogan, "Make America Great Again." This slogan has resonated with millions of American's who desire to see the USA as they once knew it return to its former glory, a nation that honored God, not on just its currency, but in its heart. However I believe in order to make America be great again, America has to make the One who made it great, great again.

George Washington was chosen unanimously as the new nation's first president without a single dissenting vote. Now once again, after wishing to end his life of service to his country and retire back to his farm, Washington again answers the call to serve his country. For George Washington was truly a man who did not seek power; in fact, he detested power. He sought personal honor. But he never sought accolades and believed in service to his country. President George Washington often wrote in a daily devotional journal. He wrote about what he felt made America great: he said, "It is impossible to rightly govern the world without God and the Bible. It is impossible to account for the creation of the universe, without the agency of a Supreme Being. It is impossible to govern the universe without the aid of a Supreme Being. It is impossible to reason without arriving at a Supreme Being.

Religion is as necessary to reason, as reason is to religion. The one cannot exist without the other. A reasoning being would lose his reason in attempting to account for the great phenomena of nature, had he not a Supreme Being to refer to."

I believe it is time for America to ask God to once again bless her. It's time for America to repent and call on the God that made her great. God speaks to us in these words found in the scriptures in book of Revelation Chapter 2: *"But I have this against you, that you have left your first love. Therefore remember from where you have fallen, and repent and do the deeds you did at first; or else I am coming to you and will remove your lampstand out of its place—unless you repent."* (NASB)

Recently my wife and I took a trip to Nairobi Kenya. It was an eye opening trip as I saw how a once third world nation, became wealthy. While there for five days I finally asked a local how Kenya became so wealthy. He said to me, "America introduced the Word of God to us and we believed, now America needs the God that they introduced to us. We have been praying for your nation to return to God." I was floored and couldn't respond. To know that we had influenced them to turn to God but now we had left our first love.
America is at a turning point, we need to remember how we first loved God, how we were founded upon Christian values and what made us so great was because we didn't mind proclaiming a great God to the world.

20 LIFE QUOTES:

Covenant

"The name of the Lord is a fortified tower, the righteous run to it and are safe." – Proverbs 18:10

"I will never break my covenant with you." – Judges 2:1

"A Covenant made with God should be regarded not as restrictive but as protective." – Russell Nelson

"I will remember my covenant which is between me and you and every living creature of all flesh; and never again shall the water become a flood to destroy all flesh". – Genesis 9:15

Marriage

"A successful marriage is an edifice that must be rebuilt every day". - Andre Maurois

"Let the wife make the husband glad to come home, and let him make her sorry to see him leave". – Martin Luther

"Marriages, like a garden, take time to grow. But the harvest is rich unto those who patiently and tenderly care for the ground". – Darlene Schacht

"Marriage is a divine covenant not a contract, don't confuse miscommunication with incompatible". –Kemmy Nola

Family

"Families are like fudge – mostly sweet with a few nuts."
- Unknown

"Everyone needs a house to live in, but a supportive family is what builds a home." - Anthony Liccione

"You don't choose your family. They are God's gift to you, as you are to them." - Desmond Tutu

"Lead your life so you wouldn't be ashamed to sell the family parrot to the town gossip." – Will Rogers

Morality

"The most important human endeavor is striving for morality in our actions. Our inner balance and even our very existence depend on it. Only morality in our actions can give beauty and dignity to our lives. – Albert Einstein

"The purpose of morality is to teach you, not to suffer and die, but to enjoy yourself and live." –Unknown

Life

"Man cannot discover new oceans unless he has the courage to lose sight of the shore." – Andre Gide

"Lay a firm foundation with the bricks that others throw at you." – David Brinkley

"The greatest mistake you can make in life is to be continually fearing you will make one." – Unknown

"Getting over a painful experience is much like crossing monkey bars. You have to let go at some point in order to move forward." – C.S. Lewis

"When nothing is sure, everything is possible".
– Margaret Drable

"New Beginnings are often disguised as painful endings."
- Lao Tzu

INVITATION

Let me introduce to you My Friend. Perhaps you are reading this and it has really been a blessing to your life but you've never come to know the Lord Jesus Christ or have invited Him into your heart. I want to help you by having you say this simple prayer.

—Lord Jesus I come to you with all my lemons in need of a Savior. I make my covenant vow to you. I give you my heart, I give you my mind, and I give you my soul and my body. This day I declare and degree to the world that I no longer belong to the kingdom of darkness but I now belong to the Kingdom of GOD!

Because of His Word I am a King's kid, therefore I am entitled to the King's benefits in Jesus Name. AMEN! Welcome to the family of the Kingdom of God!

CHRISTOPHER L. WALKER BIO

Known for his powerful and dynamic vocal ability as a worship leader, Pastor Christopher has the ability to usher in the presence of God with boldness and fervor. His preaching is humorous, direct, personal, and cuts to the core of real issues. He has an anointing to bring healing to the soul, and encourage you to reach your destiny. Pastor Chris has ministered across the country as well as abroad in South Korea, Bahamas and Africa.

His vocal gift has given him a platform on over 100 Christian radio and television networks such as TBN, CTN, Cornerstone, Impact, TCT, and Sirius XM Radio. He is a recording artist, the winner of the 2014 Readers Choice Award for his popular book, Lemons to Lemonade: Overcoming Your Past & Winning in the Now, and the winner of the 2015 Southlake Black Achievers. He is the Senior Pastor and Founder of Cathedral of Power International Church.

To schedule Pastor Chris at your Church, Conference, or Special event call today! 352-321-2930 or visit us online at cathedralofpower.org
Or write us at:
P.O. Box 120337
Clermont, FL 34712

JOIN ME ON THESE SOCIAL MEDIA NETWORKS

- **f** CHRISLWALKERSR
- **t** @PSCHRISWALKER
- **YouTube** CATHEDRAL OF POWER CHANNEL
- **in** CHRISLWALKERSR

Christopher L. Walker

ALSO AVAILABLE FROM CHRIS L. WALKER

LEMONS TO LEMONADE
OVERCOMING YOUR PAST & WINNING IN THE NOW!
AVAILABLE ON AMAZON.COM & CHRISLWALKER.COM

MIGHTY & GREAT - MUSIC CD
AVAILABLE ON I-TUNES, CDBABY.COM

www.ingramcontent.com/pod-product-compliance
Lightning Source LLC
Chambersburg PA
CBHW071203090426
42736CB00012B/2432